Kevin Gyan Baffour: UX Design Visionary

I am a prominent author and visionary in the field of User Experience (UX) design. My passion for creating intuitive digital experiences has garnered widespread recognition and admiration from UX enthusiasts worldwide. With a focus on user-centric designs and a deep understanding of human behaviour, my work emphasises usability, accessibility, and aesthetics. My contributions to the UX community continue to inspire and elevate the discipline to new heights.

Kevin Gyan-Baffour
18 Dudley Street, Colne.
https://kgbaffour.my.canva.site/ux-ui-portfolio#

Prologue

Within the walls of a care home, where age and wisdom converge, a silent struggle unfolds in the stillness of the night. Nocturnal enuresis, an unspoken challenge among the elderly residents, calls for compassion and innovative solutions. Amidst the shadows, a visionary in UX design, Kevin Gyan Baffour, steps forward, aiming to blend technology and empathy to ease the burdens and bring comfort to those who have journeyed through life's chapters. This is the tale of Managing Nocturnal Enuresis in the Elderly in a Care Home, where innovation meets humanity in pursuit of serenity.

Chapter 1

Advances in life expectancy have resulted in a significant rise in the demand for elderly care facilities, catering to those aged 65 to 95, both in residential homes and dedicated care centers. With these growing needs come a multitude of practical challenges faced by family members and caregivers within the elderly care sector. Among these challenges, urinary incontinence stands out as a prevalent issue, yet it has received little attention from the human-computer interaction (HCI) community.

In response to this gap in knowledge, the present study takes on the mission to explore and implement modern, non-invasive technologies to assist and manage this problem effectively. Through in-depth interviews with six experienced carers in the elderly care sector, a deeper understanding of the issue has been attained.

This work offers two significant contributions to the field. First, it delves into the design space, investigating various approaches and solutions to tackle urinary incontinence in elderly care. Second, a tangible outcome of this exploration emerges in the form of a prototype - a promising step towards addressing the practical challenges and enhancing the quality of life for the elderly.

Nocturnal enuresis (NE), commonly known as bedwetting, is a prevalent condition observed in children, often associated with developmental delays, physical limitations, or behavioral disorders. On the other hand, the elderly can also experience nighttime involuntary urination (urinary incontinence), which may be linked to medical complications like dementia, aging-related bladder issues, and sleep problems.

As technology continues to advance, there is growing interest in exploring non-invasive solutions for managing NE in children and addressing urinary incontinence in the elderly. The integration of modern technologies, such as the Internet of Things (IoT), holds promising potential in improving the lives of older adults residing in care homes. However, introducing technology in care homes, especially for individuals with dementia, presents unique challenges for Human-Computer Interaction (HCI) researchers.

In this context, user-centered design (UCD) plays a vital role, emphasizing the importance of actively involving users in the design process. By considering the specific needs and preferences of the elderly, technology can be tailored to meet their requirements and be more readily accepted. Factors like acceptance, user-centeredness, benefits, feasibility, reliability, and affordability are crucial for the successful implementation of technology in elderly care.

As we delve into the realm of designing for the elderly, it becomes evident that traditional UCD methods may not fully capture the complexities and nuances involved. Therefore, developing more insightful approaches tailored to the unique needs of the elderly becomes essential to create technologies that genuinely enhance their well-being and quality of life.

The primary focus of this study is to explore relevant technology to improve the quality of life for the elderly with NE (nocturnal enuresis). Opinions were collected from research papers and care domain experts to influence the ideas in this work. Faster detection of elderly individuals saturated in their beds could lead to improved health and wellbeing. The study investigated various pieces of research in regard to design ideas.

The main objectives of the study are as follows:
1. Application of user-centered techniques to understand domain requirements.
2. Exploration of the design space using user experience design approaches (UXD).
3. Creation and evaluation of a high-fidelity IoT prototype.

LITERATURE REVIEW AND RELATED WORK
The admittance of the elderly with Dementia in care homes has been increasing, and technology has been acknowledged as a tool to improve their safety, independent living, and support their day-to-day activities. There have been developments in technology for reminders, stimulation, surveillance, safety, and behavioral management.

The shortage of staff in care homes affects the quality of life for residents, and many care homes rely on carers provided by staffing agencies who may not have specific AT training for the elderly. Urinary incontinence is also a concern, and many devices have been developed for bedwetting in children, but not as much for the elderly.

Designing for the elderly should be user-centered and acceptable for users with cognitive disorders like Alzheimer's disease. Several studies have explored the use of technology for elderly safety and wellbeing, but not specifically for urinary incontinence and NE.

Some studies proposed the use of autonomous bed wetting alarms or moisture detection systems, but cost and usability issues remain. Robotic caregivers could be an alternative, but ethical issues need consideration.

There is no evidence of research into AT for aiding the elderly with urinary incontinence and NE. Absorbent pads and incontinent pads are commonly used in care homes, but there is a need for further research in this area.

The study also mentions the use of robotic caregivers, the challenges of designing for Dementia patients, and the importance of an empathetic approach in participatory designs.

Overall, this study aims to explore relevant technology to enhance the quality of life for the elderly with NE. It draws inspiration from previous research in technology use for the elderly and urinary incontinence but highlights the need for further investigation and user-centered design.

USER GROUPS
In the context of human-computer interaction (HCI), designers must consider the end-users and their needs. Three types of users are commonly identified: primary users, secondary users, and tertiary users. Primary users are the main users of the design, while secondary users are those who use the design in-between, and tertiary users are those affected by the use and purchases of the design.

DEFINING THE STUDY'S FOCUS

This study focused on a specific population: the elderly living in care homes, particularly those with Dementia who suffer from urinary incontinence. While the study did not directly involve people with Dementia, it centered on their carers as representatives. In a user-centered approach, it is essential to consider the impact of the design on all stakeholders, and carers, spending considerable time with the residents, emotionally invest themselves in their care.

STAFFING ISSUES AND NIGHTTIME CARE

A study conducted from 2010 to 2011 compared staffing levels and standards in six countries. The findings revealed that Dementia units were often understaffed during the night, which can pose challenges for the care of the elderly with nocturnal enuresis (NE).

DESIGN THINKING PROCESS

Design thinking is a systematic and innovative approach that allows designers or individuals to investigate, develop, and design prototype models, gathering feedback and iterating on the design. It is a problem-solving process that places user needs at its core, fostering creativity and innovation to achieve successful user-centered design outcomes. Designers employ various investigative tools and methods such as surveys, interviews, focus groups, and brainstorming to understand their users better. Observational techniques are significant in gaining insights into users' behaviors and feelings about a product.

In this study, the problem of elderly individuals experiencing urinary saturation was reframed using a human-centric approach. The five stages of the design thinking process, which are indispensable and should be used sequentially without skipping any, were applied to explore possible solutions. The design thinking process was subjective, and a focus group interview with carers provided valuable insights for the design process.

Overall, design thinking allows designers to develop functional ideas with meaningful impact while recognizing patterns. It involves an argumentative process where designers continually debate and refine their solutions to address the problem effectively. The design thinking process is viewed metaphorically as a system of interconnected spaces that form a continuum of innovation.

OBSERVATIONAL TECHNIQUES

In exploring potential solutions to the identified problems, an observational method was used to gain a better understanding of carers' actions and behaviors during their shifts at the care home, particularly in relation to elderly residents with urinary incontinence. The goal was to determine how carers responded to emergency buzzers and alarms and whether these notification systems effectively alerted them regardless of their locations. Observations helped identify patterns, behaviors, and reactions of carers when attending to elderly residents experiencing urinary incontinence. It was evident that carers responded promptly to emergency situations but faced challenges in providing regular checks for residents with nocturnal enuresis due to high workloads during night shifts.

EMPATHY STAGE

The design thinking process began with the empathy stage, which focused on understanding and empathizing with the users, in this case, the carers. Given the cognitive impairments of most elderly residents, consulting with experienced carers provided valuable insights into the area of concern. Observations played a crucial role in developing empathy for the users, and three design approaches were considered: how, when, and why carers interacted with the residents.

The empathetic relationship between designers and users allowed a better understanding of the carers' needs and experiences, contributing to a more user-centered design. This phase involved learning about the elderly residents in the care home and their carers through a focus group interview with six participants. The physical environment of the care home was also explored, leading to the identification of specific instances of urinary incontinence among residents with Dementia.

The design thinking process consists of multiple stages, and the empathize, define, ideate, prototype, and test stages were adapted to this study. Immersing in the physical environment and gaining insights from carers and residents were critical in addressing the problem of urinary incontinence effectively.

9. EMPATHETIC TECHNIQUES

In the design process, various tools and techniques have been described by authors to promote empathy. These techniques fall into three main categories: investigation, communication, and ideation.

Investigation: This involves direct contact between designers and users, allowing designers to understand the complex needs of users. Observational studies and generative meetings with designers, researchers, and users are recommended to gain valuable insights. In this study, direct contact with carers representing elderly residents with Dementia was crucial for understanding their needs and behaviors.

Communication: When direct contact is not feasible, communication techniques can be used to convey user findings to the design team. External researchers may conduct user studies and communicate the data to designers. Storytelling techniques such as personas, scenarios, and storyboards are useful in representing user experiences. The design process in this study involved research, organization, and the use of personas and scenarios to visualize the user journey and prototype development.

Ideation: Designers immerse themselves in the users' experiences to stimulate current circumstances and understand their needs. Techniques such as role-playing, bodystorming, and informance help gain a deeper understanding of users' perspectives. Observations of how other systems are designed and how users interact with them influence the design of the prototype, considering user notifications and the location of the buzzer to avoid disturbing other residents.

10. DEFINING THE PROBLEM

Defining the problem is a crucial stage where all relevant information gathered during previous stages is synthesized to identify underlying issues. Meaningful patterns are identified to understand user needs better. This study broke down the problem into smaller sections during the empathy stage and conducted interviews and observations with carers to gather information.

The design process incorporates key principles of Human-Centered Design (HCD), including involving users in the design process, allocating functions between users and the system, receiving feedback from users (carers), iterating designs, and using multidisciplinary design teams.

To understand user needs, personas were created based on initial research and interviews. Personas are fictitious characters representing potential users, and they help clarify and understand users' identities and goals. Scenarios were developed to analyze the problem further and aid in idea development. Personas and scenarios were shown and discussed with all participants (carers) to obtain feedback and improve the design.

The personas used in this study were developed using a prototyping tool called Xtensio, and images from Flickr were used to differentiate and recognize each persona. The personas represented different residents with varying needs and medical conditions. Scenarios were created to illustrate the interactions and motivations of each persona with the prototype.

In summary, the empathy and defining stages in the design thinking process were enriched by techniques such as personas, scenarios, and observations, allowing a better understanding of user needs and experiences to inform the development of the prototype.

11. IDEATION

The ideation stage in the design process involved exploring the literature and findings to outline the problems that needed to be solved. Understanding the users and their needs was a key aspect of this stage, encompassing both negative and positive experiences. Brainstorming sessions were conducted to generate creative ideas, focusing on the users and their requirements. In this process, quantity was prioritized over quality, encouraging thinking outside the box.

Sketching played a vital role in creating three-dimensional objects in the designers' minds. It provided a quick and iterative way to put concepts and ideas on paper without worrying about perfection. Storyboarding, which involves a sequence of illustrations and related captions, helped in capturing, communicating, and investigating the user's experience with the prototype. Storyboards presented scenarios for specific personas and allowed for easy visualization and understanding.

Storyboards were valuable in conveying user needs to stakeholders, as they provided a common visual language that people from different backgrounds could easily interpret. Incorporating realistic photos and depicting more stages in each narrative could enhance the storyline's power and communicate effectively with users and stakeholders.

The use of storyboards in the design process served several purposes:
- Visualization: Storyboards transitioned abstract ideas into infographics, making it easier to share and explain the design vision visually.
- Memorability: Storytelling in storyboards is more memorable, as sensory details and emotional elements generate stronger images that are easier to retain.
- Empathy: Storyboards with emotional characters allow users to relate to real-life situations, eliciting empathy.

- Engagement: Engaging storyboards capture readers' curiosity and keep them interested in following the narrative to its conclusion.

In summary, the ideation stage involved brainstorming, sketching, and storyboarding to explore a wide range of ideas, ensure user-centricity, and communicate the design vision effectively.

DESIGN PROCESS

The design process involved gaining insight, perception, and experiences from experts in the domain through a focus group. The focus group approach facilitated data collection by encouraging participants to interact and exchange anecdotes and viewpoints. Six participants were involved, including 2 senior carers, 2 team leaders from the Dementia unit, and 2 junior carers, with ages ranging from 19 to 58 (mean age = 35).

All participants volunteered for the interview, which lasted approximately 1 hour and 20 minutes. The focus group provided a broad scope of subjects and allowed for clarifying ideas and opinions regarding the problem of elderly individuals with Nocturnal Enuresis (NE). The diversity of participants in terms of generations was essential, as it influenced the novelty of the design.

A consent form was approved by the study supervisor, and each participant received a question guide sheet before the session. While the focus group was advantageous, it also posed challenges, as the participants used humor to avoid difficult questions due to hierarchical differences between senior and junior carers.

Data analysis involved transcribing the recorded interview independently. Focus groups were advantageous for their cost-effectiveness and speed in data collection. The location and timing of the focus group were considered, and the discussions were recorded using a smartphone. Pseudonyms were assigned to each participant during transcription to maintain anonymity.

The data analysis process was time-consuming but worthwhile, as it provided rich insights into the participants' articulated ideas and concerns. The analysis revealed a common emerging subject: the need for a system to alert carers when residents with urinary incontinence are asleep.

DATA COLLECTION

The audio recording was done using a Samsung voice recorder on a smartphone. The interviews were conducted in an office at the care home, resulting in some background noise. Transcripts of the recordings were stored securely on the university's computing systems and anonymized to protect participant identities.

A short case scenario involving a carer at Hazel Care Homes highlighted the challenges faced when attending to residents' needs, especially during emergencies. The proposed incontinence system would have been beneficial in alerting carers to attend to the residents promptly.

SCOPE OF THE PROJECT

The project's scope involved integrating a moisture sensor, conductive thread, buzzer or sounder, LCD screen, and LED bulbs connected to an Arduino Uno microcontroller. The conductive thread was stitched onto a waterproof material, and the moisture sensor would trigger the Arduino board when moisture was present. The prototype would alert carers through a low and continuous tone buzzer and LED bulbs. The components considered for the prototype included the microcontroller, moisture sensor, LED bulbs, buzzer, conductive thread, waterproof material, switch panel, jumper wires, and LCD module.

In summary, the design process encompassed conducting a focus group, analyzing data, and defining the scope of the project to develop a prototype to support elderly individuals with Nocturnal Enuresis in care homes.

7. METHODOLOGY

Designing the Notification and Detection Systems

The design of the prototype involved two systems: the notification system and the detection system. The detection system consisted of the conductive material and the moisture sensor, while the notification system included the buzzer, LED bulb, and LCD screen. Based on initial inquiries at the care home, it was observed that all the notification systems used switch panels located in the care home's lobby.

For this study, the switch panel was designed after conducting initial research into similar designs. Hardboard was chosen for the switch panel's material as it allowed for easy demonstration of the prototype. Hardboard was lightweight and could be cut with a hacksaw. Tools and materials used in the design were purchased from a local DIY store and were cost-effective.

The switch panel would be placed in the care home's foyer, accessible to both carers and managers, alongside other notification panels, such as emergency unit systems and help required panels. Wearable technology was not considered as effective for this study due to infection control guidelines for care homes. These guidelines discourage staff from wearing watches or jewelry to ensure proper handwashing before administering personal care to residents and to minimize the risk of skin tears during manual handling.

Tools Used in Designing the Switch Panel:
- Hardboard
- Retractable knife
- Hacksaw
- Ruler
- Gorilla glue
- Sanding block
- Pencil
- Screwdriver
- Scissors

Components Used:
- Jumper wires
- Plastic strips to be cut and glued into pouches
- LED bulbs
- Pieces of paper with room numbers written on them
- LCD screen

In summary, the design process involved creating two systems: the detection system and the notification system. The switch panel, designed using hardboard, was chosen for its accessibility and effectiveness in a care home setting. Wearable technology was not considered due to infection control guidelines and potential risks during resident care. Various tools and components were utilized to create the switch panel for the prototype.

Figure 1 - Tools used in designing the switch panel

The design process began with a quick and rough sketch on a piece of paper, allowing for exploration and articulation of the idea. The dimensions shown in FIG - 2 were then transferred from the paper sketch to the hardboard using a pencil and ruler.

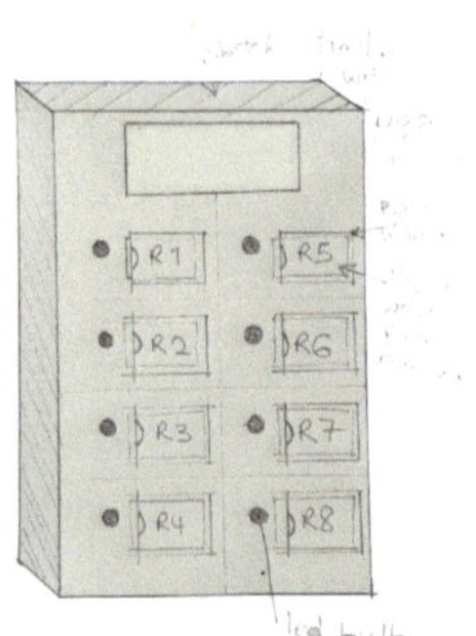

Figure 2 - Initial sketch of the switch panel

The hardboard pieces were cut into the necessary shapes and sizes and then joined together using polyurethane glue. After assembling the model, the edges were carefully cut with a retractable knife and sanded to achieve a smooth finish. Six holes were punched through the front of the model using a screwdriver, allowing for the secure placement of the LED bulbs using glue. Plastic pouches were cut to the required shapes and affixed onto the designated spaces as illustrated in FIG - 3.

Figure 3 - Assembling the switch panel

The switch panel would feature an attached LCD screen displaying the room number that requires assistance. This addition ensures that even if carers overlook the buzzer or sounder, they can easily notice the red LED light or read the message displayed on the screen. The LCD screen was securely wired and connected to the switch panel, as depicted in FIG - 4.

The detection system comprises the incontinent mat and conductive threads, while the notification system includes the LCD screen, LED bulb, and buzzer. The buzzer, LED bulb, and LCD screen would be placed inside the switch panel, which will be positioned in the care home's foyer. To identify the specific room, a replaceable piece of paper with the corresponding room number would be inserted into the plastic pouch on the switch panel.

The microcontroller and moisture sensor would be attached to the resident's bed or within their room. Finally, the incontinence mat would be placed discreetly under the bedsheet to detect moisture and trigger the notification system when necessary.

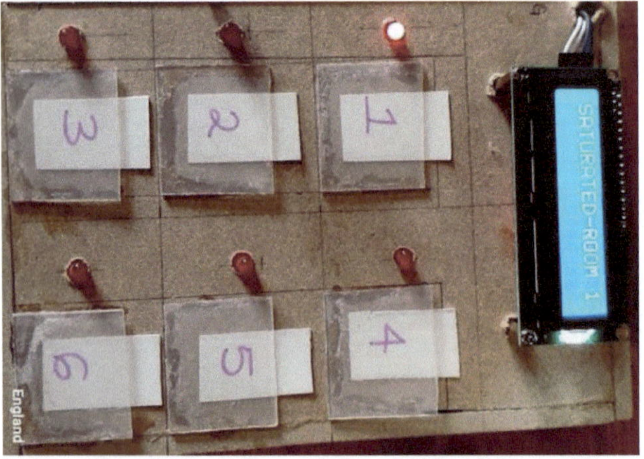

Figure 4 – Assembling of the notification system – switch panel (LCD screen and Led bulb)

Components used (Hardware) - Arduino Uno

Arduino Uno is an open-source computer hardware and software company that provides a microcontroller board used for this study (Arduino, 2015). Arduino Uno is a versatile and multi-platform tool capable of reading inputs and converting them into outputs (Fisher and Gould, 2012). Unlike other boards like Raspberry Pi and Arduino Mega, Arduino Uno is chosen for its simplicity and ease of use in creating simple prototypes. It runs only one program at a time, and once the code is uploaded onto the IDE (Integrated Development Environment), the Arduino can function independently without the need for an operating system (OS) (Junior et al., 2013). This makes it ideal for this study, where a straightforward interactive prototype is required.

Figure 5 – Arduino Uno

Moisture Sensor Module The moisture sensor board (YL-38) was used in this study and comprises of several pin-outs, controls and indicators. Below is a description of the various pinout in FIG – 6 and Table 2.

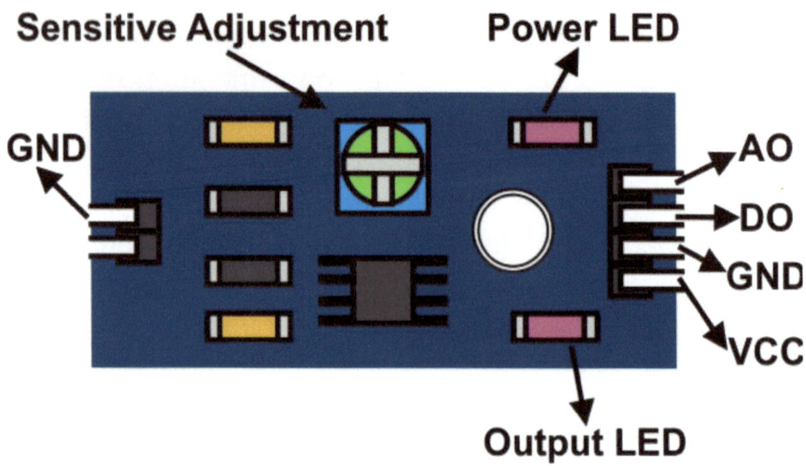

Figure 6 - Moisture Sensor (YL-83)

The YL-38 moisture sensor board incorporates an LM193 comparator chip, which compares the input from the incontinent mat's sensors to a pre-set value determined by the tiny potentiometer on the YL-38 board. When the specified value is reached, the comparator chip turns off, and this is achieved using an analog pin and Arduino codes. The

YL-38 sensor board simplifies the calibration process and its integration into the Arduino code.

How it works: In this study, the YL-38 moisture sensor is comprised of two main components: the incontinent mat (variable resistor) and the moisture sensor (electronic board). The moisture sensor module has a built-in potentiometer with sensitive adjustments for digital outputs. The conductors' shape is drawn and stitched with conductive thread to collect moisture in-between them, as depicted in FIG - 9.

The incontinent mat acts as a variable resistor, leading to a drop in resistance between the two conductors—one conductor with a positive polarity and the other connected to GND. The separation between the tracks of the conductive thread creates a short circuit whenever moisture is present on the wet conductors, as shown in FIG - 9.

The moisture sensor module, together with the incontinent mat, holds significant importance in the design for this study. The module is set up in two sections: the incontinence mat and the moisture sensor.

Table 2 - Moisture sensor module (Description)

PIN, CONTROL, AND INDICATORS	DESCRIPTION
VCC	+5 volts (power source)
GND	Ground
DO	Digital output (high or low)
A0	Analog Output
POWER LED	Power indication
OUTPUT LED	Illuminates when urine exceeds the set threshold by sensitive adjustment
SENSITIVITY ADJUSTMENT	Clockwise is more sensitive, Anti clockwise is less sensitive.

In exploring the development of the incontinence mat, several considerations were taken into account regarding the conductive material. These considerations were discussed with the supervisor of this study. Initially, aluminium foil tape was purchased from the local DIY store. The foil tape was cut into thin lines to create a separation between the conductors. These conductors were then attached to the waterproof fabric, as illustrated in FIG - 7.

Figure 7 - initial idea using conductive tape

However, this idea did not work as the aluminium tape was coated with an adhesive, rendering it non-conductive. The design of the incontinent mat was then modified and comprised the following components, as depicted in FIG - 8:

1. Waterproof fabric

2. Ruler
3. Pencil
4. Sewing needle
5. Conductive thread.

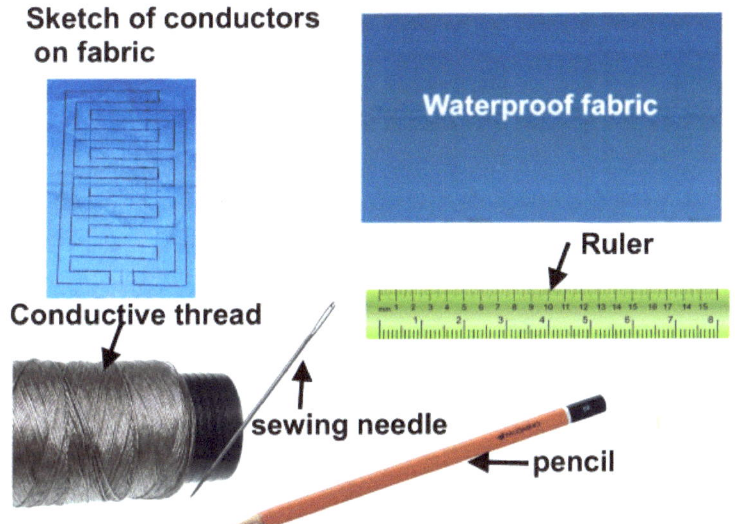

Figure 8 - Preparing the incontinence mat

The conductive thread was stitched onto the waterproof fabric (incontinence mat). Each side of the conductors was then connected to a jumper wire, as shown in FIG – 9 (A). These jumper wires were further connected to the moisture sensor, depicted in FIG – 9 (B). The entire prototype was then assembled and attached to a board for demonstration, as depicted in FIG – 10.

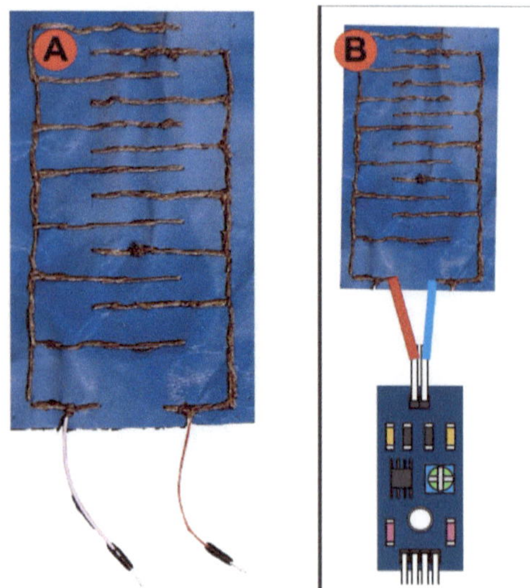

Figure 9 - (A) Conductive thread stitched onto fabric and (B) connected to the moisture sensor module.

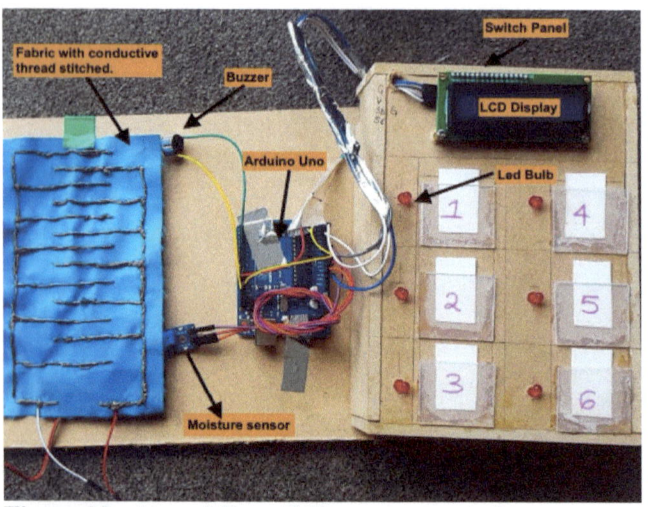

Figure 10 - Assembling all the components for demonstration

Wiring the components:

In connecting the moisture sensor to the Arduino board, the following connections were made, as shown in Table – 3. The "Voltage Collector Collector" (VCC) on the moisture sensor was connected to 5 volts on the Arduino board, while the Ground (GND) on the moisture sensor was connected to the ground on the Arduino board. The Ao on the moisture sensor was connected to the analog pin 0 on the Arduino board, and finally, the moisture sensor was connected to the incontinence mat using jumper wires.

Table 3 - Connecting the moisture sensor to the Arduino board

Moisture sensor	Arduino Uno
VCC	5 Volts
GND (Ground)	GND (Ground)
Ao	Analog in 0

The sensor module measures moisture through the analog output pins and returns a digital output when a threshold is surpassed.

Connecting the Led Bulbs:

The positive pin of the Led bulb (anode) was connected to pin 11 on the Arduino, and the shorter or negative pin (cathode) was connected to the GND pin on the Arduino. The LED bulb was programmed to light up if the incontinence mat was heavily soaked and would have to reach the threshold before the LED lights up.

Connecting the Buzzer:

The positive pin of the buzzer was connected to pin 10 on the Arduino, and the negative pin on the buzzer was connected to the GND pin on the Arduino.

Connecting the LCD Module:

The LCD was wired to the Arduino board as follows: The GND on the LCD was connected to the GND on the Arduino, and the VCC on the LCD was connected to 5 volts on the Arduino board. The SDA and the SCL on the LCD were wired to Analog pins 4 and 5 on the Arduino board, respectively. Once connected, the LCD lights up, showing that the correct connection was made.

Three files were downloaded: The scanner, the I2C address file, and the latest liquid crystal code (Zip file). The liquid crystal file would be added to the Arduino library once the Arduino IDE has been downloaded. Once the components were assembled, the Arduino IDE was downloaded and installed. The Arduino Uno is connected to a laptop using a USB 2.0. Under the tools section, the type of microcontroller is selected, as well as the appropriate serial port, as shown in FIG – 11.

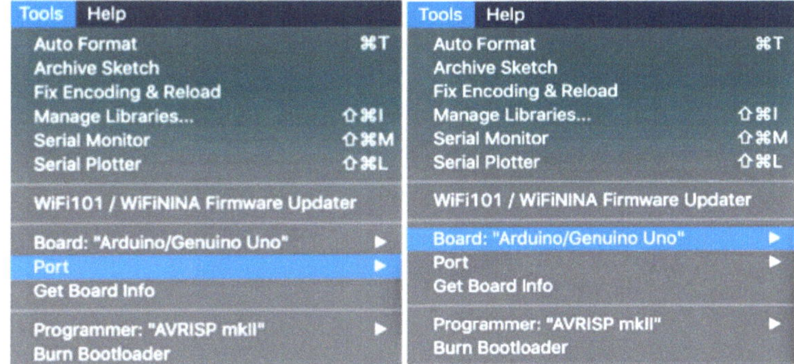

Figure 11 - Selecting Arduino board and setting the serial port

If the incontinence mat were completely soaked with moisture at the threshold, a "Heavily saturated" message would be sent to the serial monitor. This would activate the LED light and set off the buzzer. A message would also be displayed on the LCD accordingly. Once the incontinence mat has been cleaned and is dry, the LED light goes off, and the buzzer stops.

```
Incontinence_detector

int urinesense= A0; // analog sensor input pin 0
int buzzerout= 10; // digital output pin 10 - buzzer output
int countval= 0; // counter value starting from 0 and goes up by 1 every second
int ledout= 11; // digital output pin 11 - led output

void setup(){
    Serial.begin(9600);
    pinMode(buzzerout, OUTPUT);
    pinMode(ledout, OUTPUT);
    pinMode(urinesense, INPUT);
}
void loop(){
    int urineSenseReading = analogRead(urinesense);
    Serial.println(urineSenseReading); // serial monitoring message
    delay(250);// urine sensing value from 0 to 1023.
    // from heavily saturated - no dry.
    if (countval >= 35){
        Serial.print("Heavily saturated");
        digitalWrite(buzzerout, HIGH);  //raise an alert after x time
        digitalWrite(ledout, HIGH);  // led glow
    }
    //saturated for long duration rise buzzer sound
    // there is no urine then reset the counter value
    if (urineSenseReading <500){
        countval++; // increment count value
    }
    else if (urineSenseReading >500) { // if not raining
        digitalWrite(buzzerout, LOW); // turn off buzzer
        digitalWrite(ledout, LOW); // turn off led
        countval = 0; // reset count to 0
    }
    delay(1000);
```

Figure 12 the incontinence detector code

The prototype consists of four components: the incontinence mat, the microcontroller, moisture sensor, and the switch panel. Prototypes are vital in the design process as they help solve a problem, test the solution, and validate it. They can take various forms, ranging from simple sketches and storyboards to more complex developments. Prototypes should be cost-effective and easy to modify based on user feedback.

In the care home setting, each room would have an Arduino board connected to the incontinence mat placed underneath the user's bedsheet, with the switch panel located in the foyer. Two ideas were considered for connectivity: Bluetooth and Wi-Fi, but cables were used for demonstration purposes.

During testing, water was poured onto the incontinence mat, and the serial monitor displayed the results, showing dry and wet conditions. The LED bulb lit up when the mat was soaking wet, and the buzzer activated when the counter value reached the threshold of 500 (indicating heavy saturation).

Figure 13 - Dry incontinence mat

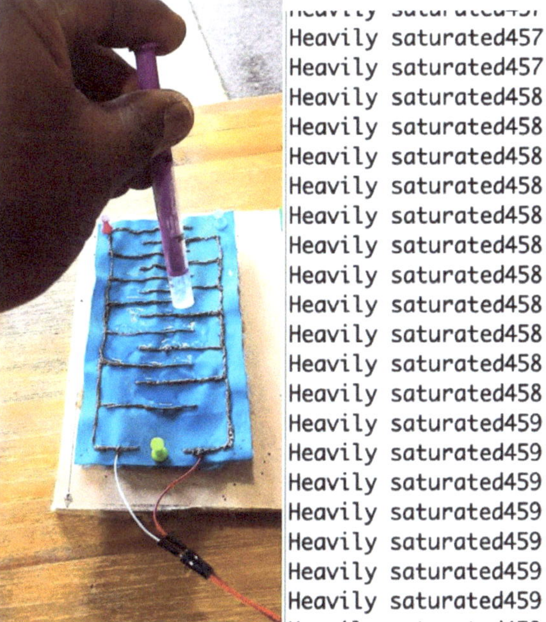

Figure 14 - Incontinence mat saturated with water

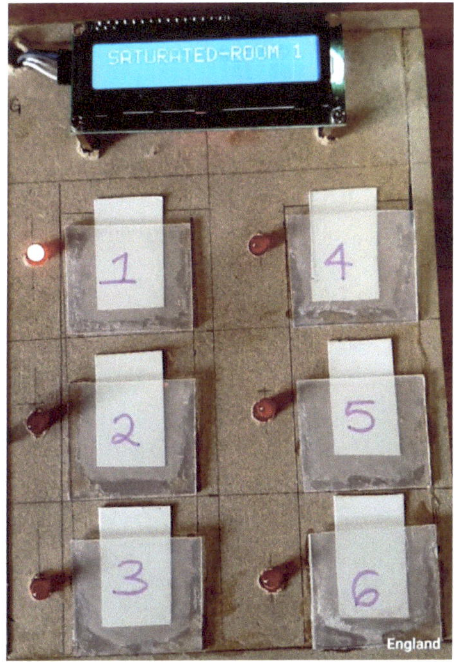

Figure 15 - LED lights up and LCD display output message

11. DISCUSSION AND LIMITATIONS

Observations and focus groups conducted at the care home provided valuable insights into the problem of Nocturnal Enuresis (NE) in the elderly. It was found that NE is associated with various conditions such as stroke, dementia, and poor mobility, leading to frustration for both residents and carers. The design process and prototype development were centered around the needs of carers and residents.

Throughout the design phases, user feedback was taken into account, addressing concerns about the location of the prototype, the tone of the buzzer, and overall safety. The evaluation process involved wetting the incontinence mat, which triggered the alarm within a short time. The prototype was considered simple, cost-effective, and durable, making it suitable for placement in each room of the care home.

However, there were some limitations to the study. The focus group should have included not only carers but also managers and deputy managers of care homes to gain broader perspectives and potential insights. Additionally, interviewing multiple care homes could have provided a more comprehensive understanding of the problem and refined the prototype design.

Despite the limitations, the exploration of technology and the design of the prototype proved effective in addressing the issue of NE in care homes. The notification and detection systems showed promising results and could be beneficial in improving the quality of care for elderly residents with urinary incontinence and NE in care homes.

12. CONCLUSIONS AND FUTURE WORK

This study explored the issue of urinary incontinence and Nocturnal Enuresis (NE) in care homes and applied User-Centered Design (UCD) techniques to design and prototype a solution. The prototype consisted of a microcontroller, sensors, and conductive thread to detect moisture levels. Various user experience techniques were employed during the design process, and the initial evaluation of the prototype showcased its potential in supporting the elderly in care homes and easing the work of carers.

The prototype included both notification and detection systems to address the needs of the elderly based on carers' requirements. Interviews and focus groups at a care home confirmed the significance of the NE issue, especially for elderly residents with Dementia who may remain saturated for extended periods. This initial approach identified key aspects for future work.

Firstly, the incontinent mat used in the study would be redesigned to incorporate a larger and more robust conductive fabric. Secondly, a mobile application would be developed to connect to the incontinence system via Wi-Fi, instantly alerting the senior carer on duty when urine is detected on the mat. This would ensure timely response to prevent residents from remaining saturated. Additionally, future work could involve measuring room temperature and humidity in each room to enhance the system further.

Lastly, fabric clips would be attached to the incontinent mat, securing it to the bedsheet to prevent accidental shifting. The prototype demonstrated the potential for a simple and cost-effective solution to address the issue of NE in the elderly.

However, due to ethical considerations, the prototype was not tested in a real-life context. Further testing and implementation in a care home setting would be essential to validate the prototype's effectiveness and potential impact on the quality of life for elderly residents with NE.

About the Author

Kevin Gyan-Baffour is a highly skilled UX/UI designer and author of UX project books. With a strong background in Graphic Design and expertise in user-centered design, web development, wireframing, and prototyping, Kevin has authored books that delve into the intricacies of UX projects. He shares his vast knowledge and practical insights through his writings, providing valuable guidance to fellow designers and aspiring professionals in the field.

Kevin's research papers are recognized for their technical expertise and hands-on approach, making them essential resources in the UX design community.